ART ATTACK

THE MIDNIGHT POLITICS OF A GUERRILLA ARTIST

Robbie Conal

ROBBIE CONAL

HarperPerennial

A Division of HarperCollins*Publishers*

To my parents' generation of true believers. And all the guerrilla posterers who gave their time, energy, and spirit. Most of all, to Debbie, Susan, and Wendy.

HarperCollins books may be purchased for educational, business, or sales promotional use. For information, please write: Special Markets Department, HarperCollins Publishers, Inc., 10 East 53rd Street, New York, NY 10022.

FIRST EDITION

ART DIRECTION DEBORAH ROSS
DESIGN CHRISTINA CHANG
ASSISTANT ROBERT VEGA
MECHANICAL PREPARATION LIBRA GRAPHICS
COLOR SEPARATIONS, PRINTING, AND BINDING IMAGO

Library of Congress Cataloging-in-Publication Data

Conal, Robbie, 1944-
    Art attack : the midnight politics of a guerrilla artist / by Robbie Conal.—1st ed.
        p.   cm.
    ISBN 0-06-096951-2 (paper)
    1. United States – Politics and government – 1981-1989 – Humor. 2. United States – Politics and government – 1989- – Humor. 3. United States – Politics and government – 1981-1989 – Caricatures and cartoons. 4. United States – Politics and government – 1989- – Caricatures and cartoons. 5. Political satire, American. 6. Political posters – United States. 7. American wit and humor, Pictorial. I . Title.
    E876.C655 1992
    973.92'0207 – dc20   92-52639

92 93 94 95 96 IS 10 9 8 7 6 5 4 3 2 1

CONTENTS

I'm a news junkie. Each morning I sit down in the studio and put off beginning my day's work by reading through three newspapers. From 1980 on, I kept bumping into stories about the Reagan administration's systematic dismantling of federal social welfare programs and its meddling in the Middle East and Central America—and found steam coming out of my eyes, ears, nose, and throat. All I could think about was the stuff these guys were doing that they *weren't* telling us about! What the hell was that pocket-junta, the Cabinet, doing to our country (and the rest of the world) in the name of representative

democracy? And who was paying their salaries, anyway? The two parties are like two old, ossified married people, looking and acting more like each other every election year. Who said two parties are enough for democracy? What about that old concept, freedom of choice in America? Gag me with the Supreme Court!

Anyway, I'd just stare at Reagan, Regan, Weinberger, James Baker III, Shultz, and Casey. Suddenly I found myself making nasty little portraits of ugly old white men with pursed lips—okay, *no lips*. And it came together—this tight little club of power-mongers were: MEN WITH NO LIPS!

These were the people who had turned ketchup into a vegetable; authorized Nancy's use of $209,508 in donations to commission a new 4,732-piece china set for the White House; and procured toilet seats at $1,000 each (built "to withstand a nuclear blast") for our submarines. What was *I* doing painting them? I could just see myself telling an art dealer, "Oh yeah, these'll be an easy sell—everyone wants a nasty little black-and-white portrait of Caspar Weinberger above the dining room table. It aids digestion!"

Painting is my medium, but it's also my livelihood, and I'm glad to show my work in galleries and sell it for as much money as I can. It would be un-American not to sell one's product and make a profit; I'm a red-blooded American boy. But these adver-

sarial portraits were emblems of abuses of power that concerned me deeply. In other words, I was pissed! Once I realized I was making art about public issues, I understood that I wasn't going to reach the public by showing my work in a commercial art gallery or museum. Art galleries are now fancy stores where you can purchase hipness and hang it like a trophy on your own wall.

And how many people can actually get to those galleries—and when are they open, anyway? The whole scene just seemed too narrowly circumscribed for what I was now doing—in terms not only of numbers, but by class and education. Working people just don't have that much free time on their hands to cruise and choose. It was time to plot my escape from the "friendly confines" of the art establishment.

Both my parents were union organizers, so I got politics with my Cheerios. As a personal focus, art was second only to baseball; I lived and died with the Brooklyn Dodgers and was just about weaned on Goya, Daumier, Kathe Kollwitz, George Grosz, and, later, John Heartfield, the great Mexican muralists, Siqueiros, Rivera, and Orozco—I gobbled them all up. My art-brat friends and I spent many happy hours of our adolescence terrorizing the guards at the Museum of Modern Art (and gaping at Picasso's *Guernica*, the centerpiece of its collection) until they'd kick us across the street, into the Donnell branch of the New York Public Library. We'd jabber our way through all the weird, sexily subversive (and hilarious) Surrealist art books until the librarians shushed us out of there.

Agitprop postering was a natural part of my home environment. The tradition of propaganda and politi-

cal postering probably goes back to a time when hairy guys scratched slogans on animal hides with burnt sticks, as in: *"We're erect, they're not,"* or *"Org is an upstanding individual, Arg is a stoop. Vote Org!"* A few eons later, Honoré Daumier would sneak into the French parliament

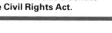

September 12, 1963. George Bush launches his first campaign for public office as a Senate candidate opposing the Civil Rights Act.

1963

1965

October 10, 1965. Ronald Reagan declares, "We should declare war on North Vietnam. We could pave the whole country and put parking stripes on it, and still be home by Christmas."

with lumps of wet clay in his pockets, sit up in the gallery and sculpt devastating little portraits of *parlementaires* he planned to satirize. Back in his studio, he moved the *maquettes* around and drew caricatures that ended up in weekly broadsheets. Occasionally, he ended up in jail after their publication. Miró made an impassioned little flyer, "*Aidez l'Espagne,*" which was actually sold on the streets of Paris for one franc to support the republican forces in the Spanish Civil War.

Of course, if you want to see great artists communicating, go to the amoral world of advertising. I did. As far as the art of persuasion is concerned, Burma-Shave wrote the book—subtle, supple, and it sells! But I *was* upset about abuses of power by public officials and I wanted to reach the public. How about just translating my paintings into posters and hitting the streets? The idea had a certain churlish charm, except for one minor drawback: I knew nothing about making posters.

So there I was, one Sunday afternoon in the summer of 1985, standing at second base, watching the other softball team run around the bases as my team, the Foul Balls, took yet another drubbing. In desperation, I leaned over, shielded my mouth with my glove, and whispered to our lefty first baseman, John Berley, "Know anything about making posters?" He offered up, "Yeah, you idiot, I'm a printer!"

We spent the next month in the back room of John's little printshop in Santa Monica, going over the rudiments of offset lithography printing. Everyone knows there are no people on the streets of Los Angeles—just cars. The posters could be a little surprise on the long drive to work in the morning: a bit of counter-infotainment, a low-level irritant, visual noise squawking away from every traffic light switching box. Like being bitten to death by ducks!

Switching boxes are crucial. They stand at eye level at every intersection—mute sentinels of the city. I got out my tape measure and sized them up for posting. But the angle of penetration had to be pre-cise. The American driving public and Angelenos in particular are accomplished surface semioticians. They can look you and your car up and down once and know your favorite restaurant, movie, and Zip Code! I wanted it to be a hybrid form, something between an *unwanted* wanted poster (*The Good, the Bad, and the Ugly*—minus the good, of course) and a tabloid newspaper front page (as in the first headline I can remember, "*We wuz robbed,*" after Bobby Thompson's home run in 1951). Maybe it would initiate a guessing game. What is it? Who is it? Who did it? And *why*?

The whole process was becoming a Tom Sawyer/ Huck Finn adventure. Especially the part where Tom tells his friends they'd really like painting that fence and they'd be real good at it, too. The asking-every-friend-you-ever-had-for-help part. This is the key to realizing any "underground" project: start small, design something modest that you can actually get done. Maybe the *next* one will be bigger and save the world.

For such a dinky job, I needed a printer with an attitude. One who might see the job as a way to humor the pressmen through a slow graveyard shift. Finally, I met Fred Gilbert, who took my money, patted me on the head, and dumped me on his foreman, Glen Gastelum, a surfer dude from Mar Vista. Glen was cool. I was a nervous wreck. My life savings ($600) were going to be run through a giant black Heidelberg press, which looked like the mutant afterbirth of the Industrial Revolution, a monster machine, fabulous and mysterious. Glen just laughed in my  face, offered me a cherry cola, and threatened to charge me double if I hung around the shop floor. The salespeople and secretaries came out of their cubbyholes to laugh at me. To my greatest embarrassment, the whole job took ten minutes. Now what was I going to do with a thousand MEN WITH NO LIPS?

1972

November 1972. Richard M. Nixon elected president. Speechwriter Raymond K. Price warns of "the sore winners problem."

1974

August 8, 1974. Richard M. Nixon resigns presidency.

1977

March 16, 1977. Congressman Dan Quayle declares that Congress should "definitely consider" decriminalizing possession of marijuana.

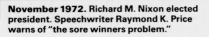

A voice whispered in the night: "Go paper-hanging, young man!" I bought gobs of glue (premixed acrylic wallpaper adhesive in five-gallon cans) at the cheapest discount hardware store I could find, and big clunky wooden wallpapering brushes—heirlooms handed down directly from Tom Sawyer and Huck Finn—and buckets galore! Then a quick call to my best friend. "Yo, Lenny, doin' anything 'round midnight?" He thought I was making a jazz joke. Poor guy. "Let's drive around one of the largest, most dangerous cities in the world, violate several municipal ordinances, and spatter ourselves with glue on street corners all night!" Now there's an offer no one with major adolescent anti-establishment fantasies could possibly refuse. Luckily, I gave him no choice.

We dubbed my Honda Civic wagon The Gluemobile, popped a little traveling music into the tape deck, and roared off into the wilds of Lalaland. I had made up a demographic plan—hit the beaches; plaster Melrose where the rockers hung out; glue the schools, UCLA, USC (that medieval walled city-state, surrounded by hostile serfs); invade downtown to entertain the nine-to-five white-collar warriors; stick it to the art museums just for fun. Make a pit-stop at King Taco in "East Los"—I wish I had the money to make a Spanish version, HOMBRES SIN LABIOS. It was scary out there. And big. We put five hours and 100 miles on The Gluemobile that night.

The posters played okay on the streets. At 1:30 a.m. in Beverly Hills I had a lovely chat with a very large man in a blue suit. He said his dog was wondering what I thought I was doing to city property. I looked (way) up at him, then over to his car. It had "K-9" stenciled on the passenger-side door and pretty, flashing red, white, and blue lights above the roof. Oh, a *police* dog. I told him that it was an art project for school, my dad was driving me around, and it really was time for me to be getting to bed. The dog didn't buy it. I suggested this was a consciousness-raising, grassroots-citizenship kind of thing. He

"HYPOCRISY IS A QUESTION OF DEGREE."

DONALD REGAN

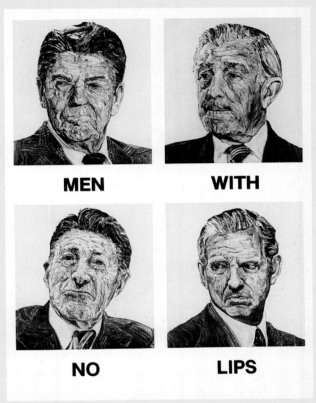

MEN **WITH**

NO **LIPS**

put his hand on my shoulder. "Let me raise your consciousness, citizen. Get your ass off my beat."

Our best moment was around 3:00 a.m. Some rockers came roaring down La Cienega in a '65 rag-top Mustang, stopped at the light, and yelled out, "Those are nasty! Are they a new band? Where are they playing?" I told them the group had had a steady gig at the White House for the past six years.

March 9, 1981. Vice-President George Bush tells *Business Week*, "Government regulations impose an enormous burden on large and small business in America, discourage productivity, and contribute substantially to our current economic woes."

1980

1981

November 4, 1980. Reagan elected president at 8:15 p.m. EST.

9

WOMEN WITH TEETH

What began as morbid curiosity about how Nancy Reagan exercised her "power behind the throne" in the White House became an ironic meditation on how differently men and women accumulate and express power. Men still have the major share of power. They sit behind huge desks—the larger the furniture, the larger the size of their operative organ—look stern, make big decisions, delegate authority, and deny pay raises. Women have had to be more circuitous and circumspect.

In my mind, I saw Nancy at a spiffy White House function in her crisp Adolfo power suit and neck chains, working the room behind that cartoon smile, teeth clenched. "Hi! How *are* you? *Sooo* nice to see you!" Burrrrr! People still ask me to explain how WOMEN WITH TEETH relates to MEN WITH NO LIPS. I tell them that Nancy Reagan bit Donald Regan's lips off.

Margaret Thatcher was the Iron Maiden and Jeane Kirkpatrick the ideological mother of the New Right. Patrick Buchanan—whose campaign slogan in the 1992 New Hampshire primary was "Warning, I don't brake for liberals!"—is her most virulent spawn. This portrait is the only known image of her smiling. Now you know why.

September 4, 1981. The Department of Agriculture proposes reclassification of ketchup and pickle relish as vegetables.

September 11, 1981. Nancy Reagan spends $209,508 in donated funds on a 4,732-piece china set. "It's badly needed," she explains.

October 4, 1981. Marine Corps Major Oliver L. North is assigned to White House duty with the National Security Council.

> # "I don't think most people associate me with leeches. But I know how to get rid of them. I'm an expert at it."
>
> **NANCY REAGAN**

As I was throwing paint at Nancy, I happened to catch her appearance on "Joan Rivers." They looked *exactly* alike. I thought about Joan and the power of the entertainment industry. I remember her from the Greenwich Village days—politically progressive, hanging out with Lenny Bruce and Woody Allen. Over the years, she had changed just about every part of her person—nose, teeth, face, politics—in her quest for success. She belonged in the poster!

On the streets, WOMEN WITH TEETH surprised me. MEN WITH NO LIPS had gone according to plan. The reaction from confused passersby was, "What the hell *is* that and what's it doing *there*?" I had found more guerrilla recruits for the WOMEN postering, so we got a little better street coverage—and a different response. In Venice, at about 1:30 a.m., I was in mid-glue-stroke (and a total mess) when a couple dressed in shredded black things with zippers and buckles got out of their Saab 900 Turbo and said in unison, "Uh-oh!" and asked for one. I agreed, if they'd explain their reaction. The woman began, "We saw MEN WITH NO LIPS. We couldn't believe it . . ." The man finished, "But when we saw *another* one, we went, 'Uh-oh We got it—somebody's got a plan . . .'"

December 30, 1981. Reagan officials seek repeal of regulations on sanitation, safety, and contagion in nursing homes.

1982

February 9, 1982. George Bush denies using phrase "voodoo economics" and challenges "anybody to find it." NBC's Ken Bode broadcasts 1980 tape of quote.

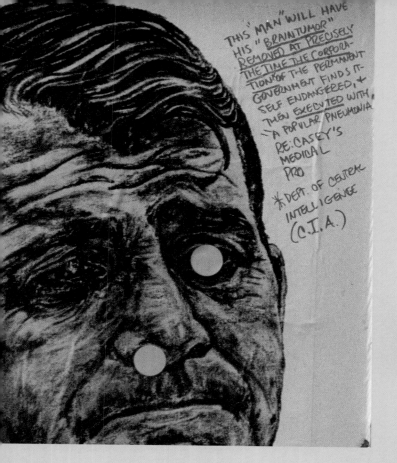

SPEAK

Donald Regan said, "Hypocrisy is a question of degree." Yeah, right. Secretly selling arms to terrorists. Using the profits to support illegal military operations in another part of the world and circumnavigating Congress and the American people in the name of representative democracy. What kind of degree was he talking about? These people had Ph.D.s in Hypocrisy.

I picked up a piece of charcoal and let the dust fly. My first poster about a specific current event would be an extravaganza! The American public knows what's going on. We just don't have an adequate system of accountability that works. But I knew that if I addressed the issues, people on the streets would understand. Reagan was in deep denial; nobody had told *him* anything about the arms for hostages/arms profits for contras schemes. I'd turn his deaf ear to the action with the caption: HEAR. Poindexter,

Reagan's national security adviser, who supposedly turned a blind eye to his subordinates' activities, would come next—peering at Ollie through his impenetrable trifocals: SEE. Ollie really wanted to tell us everything, but in the interest of "national security," he just couldn't. "Trust me, you're better off not knowing." I drew that hangdog expression, mouth firmly shut: SPEAK. Thinking Ollie's story would be the most useful information we could get, I picked SPEAK to print.

We started postering in the fall—our own little October surprise. Then I got a bright idea. There must be hardware stores in Manhattan that sell glue and brushes. My friends there had nothing to do; they'd just love to come postering around town in the middle of the night (in the dead of winter)! Come to think of it, Washington, D.C., was just an Amtrak ride away; Chicago wasn't too far, either. The first

May 6, 1982. Daryl Gates suggests African-American "veins or arteries do not open as fast as they do in normal people," thus the disproportionate number of deaths or injuries due to police choke holds.

June 1982. Explaining the murder of four nuns in El Salvador by American-supported security forces, Ambassador Jeane Kirkpatrick says, "They were not just nuns... they were political activists on behalf of the Frente."

¡RACISTAS, RAMBO-AMERICANOS GOBERNANTES DE AMERICA:

TODO LES VA A CAER ENCIMA!

Elect... LT. COL. OLLIE NORTH ☆ FOR PRESIDENT ☆

HE'LL GET THE JOB DONE!

SPEAK

SPEAK

garage-band style, no budget, total loss, rock'n'roll poster tour was under way.

After postering Austin with the help of the local art and rock scene (including Tammy, the Suburban Guerrilla—I'm glad she's on *our* side), I was off to Houston, where my guardian angel turned out to be a lovely young woman in bell-bottoms and love beads. Her Volkswagen Beetle was too small and unreliable, so we changed cars and picked up our crew. A photographer, George, came along wearing roller skates, three cameras, and a torn black T-shirt with "Urban Animals" scrawled across the front. We all stuffed into a 1978 white Mercedes diesel sedan and roared off into the urban jungle.

We were out for three nights, including pit-stops at every underground bar in town and a few places we'd have been better off avoiding, as it turned out. Like the wealthy suburbs of Houston. We rolled

downtown at about 2:00 a.m. Dozens of dark figures were jumping, whirling, *skating* around the post–oil crash haunted high rises. "They're the Urban Animals!" cried George—a motorcycle gang on roller skates. They made me an honorary member. The "Ladies' Auxiliary" tore up a T-shirt for me to wear and helped with the "roller-postering."

By the third night I was bleary and bored, but volunteers always have a hidden agenda. This crew had the hots for the wide open spaces of ranch-style homes, mowed lawns, and pastoral church cemeteries. A little class warfare. How could I refuse? The mayor of Houston, Kathy Whitmire, took exception. She threatened to fine me—or *anybody*—per poster, per day until they all came down. The posters are biodegradable. I was off to Chicago.

1983

August 3, 1983. Poverty rate rises to 15 percent, highest level since mid-sixties.

December 10, 1983. Bush meets secretly with Manuel Noriega at Panama City Airport.

1984

January 23, 1984. Reagan nominates Meese as attorney general.

13

ATE NEWS/FINAL ST

Dow Down 13 on Slow

From Times Wire Services

e stock market moved lo

verage of 30 industrials c

Exchange volume was ab
th 158.98 million shares M

Tables in

und in West

diterranean fruit fly has
s neighborhood, setting
an 81-square-mile area

missioner Paul Engler s
Los Angeles County si
n Beverly Hills in Novem
immediate cause for a
sure, 1,349 traps were
checked on a daily basis

an Hold Trad

s (*P*)—The Soviet Union
t high-level economic ta
Islamic revolution. An Iranian leader said in
with Moscow is one of Iran's top foreign polic
Tehran's official Islamic Republic News A
n Nicosia, quoted Mines and Metals Ministe
s saying his country wants to expand ties w
ncluding the Soviet Union. But the agency
owerful Parliament Speaker, Hashemi Rafs
g Moscow for supplying weapons to Iraq, Ir
ersian Gulf War, and for occupying neig

Costa Rica Envoy

ASHINGTON (*P*)—The U.S. ambassad
ewis Tambs, has resigned his post and will
he is a tenured pr

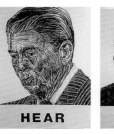

HEAR

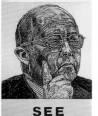

SEE

SPEAK

SPEAK

"These people want me, but they can't touch me because the Old Man loves my ass."

OLIVER NORTH

April 8, 1984. Reagan administration refuses to recognize the World Court's jurisdiction over the mining of Nicaraguan harbors.

April 9, 1984. Barry Goldwater protests mining to William Casey: "This is an act violating international law. It is an act of war."

April 25, 1984. James Baker III, asked if he's ever been to a communist country, replies, "Well, I've been to Massachusetts."

Poindexter, North, Secord Take the 5th in Iran Probes

Resentment and Mystery Increasing

From Times Wire Services

WASHINGTON—Two of President Reagan's recently departed national security aides—both still active-duty military officers—refused to publicly answer questions today from a House committee trying to explore the Iranian-contra arms-and-money connection.

The dramatic invocations of Fifth Amendment rights by Vice Adm. John M. Poindexter and Marine Lt. Col. Oliver L. North were

Lt. Col. Oliver L. North, left, and former National Security Adviser John M. Poindexter listen to questions befo[re] Committee. Both invo[...]

NEW YORK POST
Saturday, May 16, 1987   35 cents
FINAL

PANTYSCAM FUROR!

Angry Fawn: *'I never smuggled secrets in my undies for Ollie'*
PAGE TWO

FAWN HALL: "It's untrue, it's outrageous — and it's sexist!"

OLIVER NORTH: Accused of coverup.

The tragic last days of Rita Hayworth
Pages 4 & 5

May 22, 1984. On the subject of possible secret funding of the contras, Reagan declares, "Nothing of that kind could take place without the knowledge of Congress."

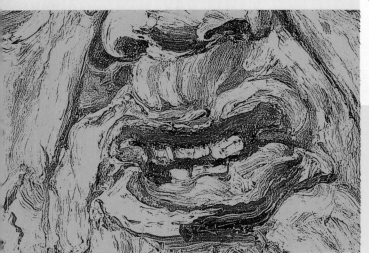

SOMETHING MEESEY

"Ebenezer Scrooge had his faults, but he wasn't unfair to anyone."

EDWIN MEESE

Ed Meese and I go way back . . . as far as People's Park, in Berkeley, '69. He was Governor Ronald Reagan's Chief of Staff when troops were firing tear gas at the Free Speech Movement. Arresting hippies for, well, just being themselves. "Easy Ed" had been busy lately—becoming the first attorney general to be investigated by three special prosecutors (in '84 for unethical receipt of loans, the Wedtech influence-peddling scandal, and his "handling" of the Iran-contra investigation). Meese just had too many fish to fry, and something started smelling real bad in the pan. Was it SOMETHING FISHY or something Meesey?

Out on the streets with SPEAK, I had noticed the posters were picking up a lot of graffiti. Everybody had something to say about Ollie. Comments, addendums, alterations, and improvements. I welcomed the participation. Positive *and* negative. Heaven for-

bid anybody should agree with me! Ed Meese even inspired my own guerrillas to add editorial comments. We found fertile background material everywhere we went, especially at construction sites. "Wild" postering of entertainment industry products, however illegal, is big business. After the adrenaline rush of the first hour's postering wore off, the hipper guerrillas would get restless. They looked for specific posters to glue SOMETHING FISHY over, so that the text of the advertisement would support our message—entertaining themselves and the more attentive passersby with the serendipitous secondary meanings. It became a little contest and something of a guerrilla tradition. Which postering crew could come up with the most sardonic pairing? The winner was *Jaws II*, *The Revenge*. Meese the Blowfish meets the big white shark!

May 30, 1984. Eight people are killed, including three international journalists, in an attempt to assassinate contra leader Eden Pastora in Costa Rica.

September 12, 1984. Regarding his failure to recall that he once supported abortion, Bush defends his credibility: "There are an awful lot of things I don't remember."

Ronald Reagan was contradicting himself all over the place. One day he "couldn't remember" authorizing contra aid; another, "It was my idea all along." And, of course, he *was* a contradiction! Government for and by the people? Ronnie sanctioned illegal covert operations all over the globe. We had a president who not only disregarded Congress, he forgot about it! Time to bore into his head, before he bored us to death—or, to put it another way, perform a little operation of my own: surgically deconstruct his utterances. I put CONTRA above, DICTION below. If I made him look a little confused and, perhaps, paranoid—that was exactly how he had made me feel for the past six years. Embrace the contradictions! When my printer finally admitted that, for a mere $200 extra, I could print black plus any solid color of my choice, I picked yellow and went off on another crusade. Even behind a mug like Reagan's,

October 12, 1984. Reagan signs legislation containing the Boland Amendment barring U.S. personnel from involvement in military resupply of the contras.

November 6, 1984. Reagan reelected president at 8:01 p.m. EST.

1985

January 28, 1985. Lawyers for Ed Meese, who is again nominated for attorney general, reveal that the Office of Government Ethics found him in violation of federal ethics standards.

18

CONTRA

DICTION

"ABORTION IS ADVOCATED ONLY BY THOSE PERSONS WHO HAVE THEMSELVES BEEN BORN."

RONALD REAGAN

that sunshine yellow would perk up any environment. I was into "urban beautification."

My guerrilla volunteers were growing. In Los Angeles we set up our midnight rendezvous at Canter's Delicatessen—open twenty-four hours, centrally located, and cheap. The only waitress who would put up with us saved four booths tucked way in the back, near the Kibbutz Room bar (this was a full-service deli). I had loaded up The Gluemobile with twenty rolls of fifty posters each, a two-gallon bucket of glue, and a brush for each team. The troops meandered in from all corners of the city—entertainment industry producers, writers and actors, college professors, students, scraggly rockers, and all shades of artists, from sculptors to graphic designers to graffiti writers. As we cranked up on kosher coffee, danishes, and cheesecake, I pulled out my handy *Thomas Guide* city map book (in L.A. no one leaves home without it). We divided up the town. Each team of two or three would take a neighborhood they felt comfortable plastering. I handed out the phone number of my favorite bail bondsman and gave a little speech about "guerrilla etiquette": Be polite to everyone, especially the police; don't poster on merchants' windows, occupied buildings, or mailboxes. If people ask for a poster, give them one. If they ask for ten, give them one. If they want to discuss the issues, talk with them, but not too long. Don't argue. Stuff like that. The object of the action was alternative distribution—sharing our concerns about public issues, not troublemaking. As for not getting caught: Don't poster in a straight line. Zigzag around your turf. Don't stay at one site for more than five minutes, or out on the streets for more than an hour and a half. This was supposed to be *empowering*, not incarcerating. Not that anyone would ever listen. These were guerrillas, and this was supposed to be the land of the free.

March 4, 1985. Congressmen McCollum and Hyde meet with North and McFarlane to discuss illegal third-country aid for the contras. Both later serve in Iran-contra investigation.

1986

January 1986. Senator Quayle of the Armed Services Committee discusses corruption in Pentagon procurements: "In the past we have tried too much to prevent the making of mistakes."

"I was very

"I DIDN'T KNOW ABOUT

definitely involved

ANY DIVERSION OF FUNDS

in the decisions

TO THE CONTRAS."

about support to the

RONALD REAGAN, March 4, 1987

freedom fighters.

It was my idea

to begin with."

RONALD REAGAN,
May 16, 1987

January 17, 1986. Reagan signs off on sale of arms to Iran and the order for the CIA not to tell Congress, but does not read two-and-a-half-page memo justifying policy.

January 13, 1986. Lee Atwater describes Reagan's antidrug campaign as "the epitome of the fad issue...it came and went in three weeks, max."

April–May 1986. Meese obstructs U.S. Attorney Leon Kellner in Miami from seeking indictments against key figures in arms smuggling to the contras.

FALSE

PROFIT

I always thought Jim and Tammy were just a joke. Kitschy, camp, Technicolor characters bounced off the wrong satellite dish, beamed in from another planet. Maybe a cosmic sitcom about silly humans, something about worshiping false eyelashes. But I was wrong.

Running around the country in the middle of the night has its educational aspects. I learned, for instance, that the United States isn't just Los Angeles and New York. And I can't tell you how many people came up to me on the streets, in all-night diners and coffee shops, and insisted on talking about Jim and Tammy. Televangelism is powerful stuff. Jim and Tammy's betrayal of their constituency's trust wasn't that far away from the Reagan administration's

abuses of its power. In fact, the Fundamentalist Christian movement was a large part of Reagan's power base. I really saw the light when Pat Robertson took a short hop, skip, and jump from his TV pulpit on the 700 Club to the Republican presidential primary race (and did very well for himself, thank you). I did a painting of Jimmy Swaggart, BLOW HARD, designed to simulate the cover of a Gideon Bible; the kind you find in Motel 6's around the country. Which is exactly where you'd find Jimmy.

Washington, D.C., is site-specific for most of my subjects. It's also the most dangerous postering turf in the country. Five different police forces patrol the Capitol Hill gridiron. The annual Washington for Jesus convention was coming up at Easter. Hmmm . . .

May 30, 1986. La Penca lawsuit filed in federal court in Miami.

June 23, 1986. Roy Cohn disbarred by New York State court, citing "unethical . . . unprofessional . . . [and] particularly reprehensible" misconduct dating back to the sixties.

June 27, 1986. World Court finds U.S. support of contras violates international law.

MAKE CALIFORNIA COUNT!

★ Jesse ★
Jackson
FOR PRESIDENT
VOTE · JUNE 7

RUBBISH
HAULING
(213) 281-1963

FALSE PROFIT

FALSE   PROFIT   PROFIT   FALSE

OPENS MAY 20
AMC CENTURY CITY

OPENS MAY 20
AMC CENTURY CITY

OPENS MAY 20
AMC CENTURY CITY

OPENS MAY 20
AMC CENTURY CIT

July 16, 1986. "Are the women of America prepared to give up all their jewelry?" asks Donald Regan, questioning support for economic sanctions against South Africa.

August 2, 1986. Roy Cohn dies at fifty-nine of AIDS.

October 5, 1986. Eugene Hasentus is shot down on a contra supply run and captured by Sandinistas.

October 10, 1986. Bush states U.S. had no link to Hasenfus plane, "directly or indirectly."

"THE ONLY WAY I CAN QUIT THINKING IS BY SHOPPING."

TAMMY FAYE BAKKER

FALSE   PROFIT

my crack metro squad of urban guerrilla posterers, an assortment of lawyers, wayward congressional aides, and photojournalists, decided to make like Easter bunnies. Decorate the Mall with colorful posters of Jim and Tammy—those rotten eggs!

It was midnight urban "beautification" to the max—except for one detail. Intent on our mission, we broke one of my cardinal rules: Don't poster in a straight line. I looked in the rearview mirror of our green 1980 Plymouth Duster and noticed we had attracted a convoy of celebrants. I'd never seen so many pretty flashing lights. The federal park police

were not amused. We all piled out of the car, handed over our driver's licenses, and watched the paddy wagons roll in. Our photographer, a red diaper baby, started speaking in tongues. It must have been biofeedback—he was allergic to police. We were ordered to clean up the Mall. The young lawyers and congressional aides must have seen their careers flashing before their eyes. Or, perhaps, just the headline in the *Washington Post* the next day. After an hour's worth of lectures, we were released. Just because the "parkies" don't have a sense of humor doesn't mean they're dumb. They know yuppies gone

October 13, 1986. Joan Rivers explains the "surprise" element she hopes to offer on her new show might be somebody admitting she is a lesbian.

October 20, 1986. Hasenfus claims Bush was aware of contra connection.

October 31, 1986. *New York Times*/CBS poll: 1 percent believe Reagan administration always tells truth; 53 percent believe it's only some (not most) of the time; 9 percent say it's hardly ever.

"WHERE IN THE BIBLE DOES IT SAY THAT A CHURCH HAS TO BE NON-PROFIT?"

JIM BAKKER

bad when they see them. We promised to go straight home to file our federal income tax returns.

About two hours later, we rolled up to an inner-city construction site wall. It was painted orange. Tammy would look so pretty on orange. A squad car pulled up alongside the Duster—city cops! They peered into the back seat. "Are those Jim and Tammy Bakker?" Yes, officer; why do you ask? "Hey, look at this, Joe. It's those FALSE PROFIT posters we've seen around tonight." Heaven help us all. "Hey, kids, can we have two to go with no glue for the station house?" No problem, officer. Say Amen, somebody!

November 13, 1986. Reagan tells TV audience, "We have not—I repeat, did not—trade weapons or anything else for hostages, nor will we ever."

November 18, 1986. *Los Angeles Times* reports 79 percent reject President's explanation of Iran deal.

December 9, 1986. North and Poindexter invoke Fifth Amendment and refuse to testify before House Foreign Affairs Committee.

1987

1987. Senator Quayle introduces special tax break for golf pros.

"NO MATTER HOW HARD WE TRIED TO DISPROVE THE RUMORS ABOUT THE CONTRAS AND DRUGS, THE STORIES NEVER WENT AWAY."

OLIVER NORTH

January 20, 1987. *New York Times* reports contra arms crews said to smuggle drugs.

January 26, 1987. Reagan tells Tower Commission he authorized arms sales to Iran in August 1985, contradicting Regan's testimony.

January 28, 1987. George Bush discusses arms sales to terrorists on morning TV. "On the surface . . . you'd have to argue it's wrong, but it's the exception that proves the rule."

My studio in Venice was a converted two-car garage, with clamp-on lights, a hot plate, and a phone machine. Each morning, before reading my stack of newspapers, I'd put up water for coffee and check the messages. I had a call from a vice president of William Morris, one of the largest talent agencies in the entertainment industry. "Please call back. We have a very important bit of business to discuss." Gee, lady, I didn't even know I had a business.

After three cups of high-octane espresso at the Rose Café, we were best friends. Which meant, of course, can you do something for free? She invited me to an introductory meeting of the Friends of the Christic Institute, at which, she promised, "Everything will be revealed." I'm into revelations. I went.

I found out that the Reagan administration hadn't just supplied the contras behind the backs of Congress and the American people. They had hired private contractors to work with members of North's secret team to transport ammunition into Nicaragua *and* fly cocaine out of Central America to defray costs. Just the latest caper of a shadow government hit squad dating back through the October Surprise, before Vietnam, perhaps to the Kennedy assassination. The Christic Institute, a nonprofit, god-squad, young lawyers for justice group, was bringing a civil suit against twenty-nine individuals connected with this "Enterprise," and the La Penca bombing in Costa Rica. Very few of us had even heard of the Christics or the "Enterprise," and even we longstanding conspiracy freaks couldn't have imagined this nefarious view of smuggling as foreign policy—cloak-and-dagger capitalism. Maybe it was just too corny to be real. Like a bad X-rated TV movie script: Dirty Harry and Rambo do Central America. But real people were dying.

The meeting was at a private screening room in

![Poster showing a skull in military uniform against a camouflage background with the words "CONTRA" above and "COCAINE" below]

Venice. I didn't know a soul in that darkened room, but I found a seat by the light of the brightest smile I'd ever seen. My first revelation of the evening: That glow belonged to a beautiful graphic designer—clearly a sign. We were put on the "poster committee." Six of us would meet once a week to try to come up with a shocker of an image that would be put up around the country, guerrilla style.

Artists don't do much in the way of cooperative creation. Most painters, myself included, never really get past staying in their rooms and playing with their

Circulation: 1,103,656 Daily / 1,368,405 Sunday   Wednesday, November 26, 1986   CC†/92 Pages Copyright 1986/ The Times Mirror Company **Daily 2**

Poindexter Resigns, North Is Fired

Leave as Meese Says Contras Got Iran Arms Funds

Less Price Control

Buy, Enjoy Is New Ethic for Chinese

By JIM MANN,
Times Staff Writer

PEKING—It is a typical Thursday night in the Yueyou (Happy Friend bar and cafe) in the center of Peking. Stevie Wonder's "I Just Called to Say I Love You" is playing in the background, and all the tables and booths are occupied.

The crowd is entirely Chinese. Many are well-dressed young professionals. Some of them have wandered in from the concert hall next door. They are doing something their parents' generation never would have dreamed of doing—blowing a bit of their own money on beer, wine and night life.

A few blocks away, in the state-owned Modern Times cocktail lounge, He Wenzhong, a well-tailored official at Radio Peking, sips from his can of Japanese Asahi beer and explains his philosophy of

President Reagan as he yielded the podium to Atty. Gen. Meese after announcing shake-up in staff.

Associated Press

Not Fully Informed About Initiative, Reagan Asserts

By JACK NELSON and ELEANOR CLIFT, *Times Staff Writers*

WASHINGTON—President Reagan accepted Vice Adm. John Poindexter's resignation as his national security adviser Tuesday and dismissed Lt. Col. Oliver L. North, a Poindexter aide, after a Justice Department investigation disclosed that as much as $30 million in proceeds from arms sales to Iran had been diverted to Nicaraguan rebels despite congressional ban on such military assistance.

Atty. Gen. Edwin Meese III, who has been investigating the Iranian arms deal, said that North was the only government official with full knowledge of the diversion of funds to the *contras* fighting the Marxist Sandinista government in Nicaragua.

Poindexter, Meese said, knew "that something of this nature was occurring" several months ago—when the congressional ban on U.S. assistance to the contras was still in place—but did not inform the President.

A government source also said it was North, acting in the face of a

**Meese, Reagan texts, Page 7.
Other stories, photos, Pages 4, 5, 6, 8 and 9.**

Associated Press

Lt. Col. Oliver L. North

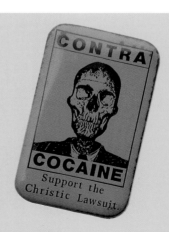

February 27, 1987. Inquiry finds Reagan and chief advisers responsible for "chaos" in Iran arms deals.

February 28, 1987. Bush acknowledges effort to swap arms for hostages.

March 7, 1987. Meese acknowledges interceding for Wedtech. *Wall Street Journal* reports rising criticism of his legal advice in Iran-contra.

crayons. But we all would like to do *something* cooperative and constructive—like playing team sports, having a family, becoming a member of Ralph Kramden's Raccoon Lodge, maybe even, heaven forbid, joining a political party. The last thing we'd consider is cooperative art! This was going to be a challenge.

Now this may sound morbid, but drawing skulls is one of the great pleasures for any artist who draws people. There's so much fun noodling to do in rendering the noggin. Any excuse will do. And this was a great one. Skulls are big in Central American culture. Day of the Dead imagery—skeletons rattle all over Mexico, Central and South America! Sugar skulls are sold on the streets for a penny a piece. Posada, one of the greatest artists in Mexican history, produced political broadsides featuring *calaveras*—skeleton figures with skull faces that satirized the prominent politicians of his time. We put our own designer version of contra camouflage behind that smiling skull, then dressed him in a Reagan administration/CIA pinstriped suit. We wouldn't want to leave anyone out in the cold.

Local Christic Institute support groups around the country managed to slap up about 10,000 posters in eighteen cities in one night! I have no idea how effective we were in raising public awareness of the Christic lawsuit. But the poster committee had a blast! So . . . artistic cooperation has its compensations. I eventually married the lady with the smile, who still designs all my best work. And "Smiley" made me very popular with the skateboarders on Venice beach. CONTRA COCAINE had everything they held dearest: skulls, camouflage, and speed.

March 24, 1987. Jimmy Swaggart admits initiating investigation of Jim Bakker's sexual conduct.

March 19, 1987. CIA reported to give contras detailed profiles of civil targets.

IT CAN'T HAPPEN

George Bush wanted to be president. He was the ultimate pinstriped suit—only the tip of his dorsal fin rippling that gray flannel surface. Bush, whose ad-libs were written by committee, was an organization man to the point of invisibility—a spook. In fact, he had run the CIA for a year. Can you imagine handing over executive privilege to the CIA?

My first reaction was, IT CAN'T HAPPEN HERE. When we hear that phrase, we know that it means just the opposite. Assume something won't happen—it will. Ignore it—it'll jump up and bite your nose off. In other words, take democracy for granted, you'll get George Bush! Sinclair Lewis even wrote a book about this in 1935. A cautionary tale about totalitarianism coming to America through the political process, a great, probably unread classic. Its title: *It Can't Happen Here.*

I'd present George with an anticampaign poster. Hey, we're patriotic; Debbie designed a lovely red, white, and blue pattern. And the Republican party convention was in New Orleans. I could take it down to the most foreign city in the United States (somewhere between Kingston and Casablanca) and entertain all the delegates! Oh, one more thing—IT CAN'T HAPPEN HERE refers to George's *inoperative* organ—the HERE is placed squarely on his brain.

This was going to be the most dangerous strike yet. I took my best organizer along for the ride—the hard-driving, high-living Patti McGuire. Patti always comes postering in uniform: oversized black leather jacket with zippers and buckles, Public Enemy T-shirt, Fishbone cap, Christian Dior "Holiday Red" lipstick, and homemade "Patti Party" tapes, a little travelin' music! Our New Orleans tour guide, Mike Swindle, was a tall, goateed, Vietnam-generation poet. A true son of the South; denizen of the blues-lounge underbelly of the French Quarter. He had us covered like red beans on rice. Glue, brushes, a Rent-A-Wreck '82 Mercury Cougar four-door sedan, and our very own posse. A veritable gumbo of guerrillas: elementary schoolteacher, mad antiques dealer, tribal art gallery owner, assorted musicians, including a whole "swamp pop" band, and sundry local artists, dropouts, and misfits from Tulane University. Our kind of people— just a tad irritated that

May 11, 1987. Meese becomes first man to be investigated by three different special prosecutors.

May 5, 1987. Iran-contra hearings begin.

May 6, 1987. William Casey, former director of CIA, dies of pneumonia.

May 15, 1987. Senator Heflin claims that Fawn Hall smuggled papers out of the White House in her underwear.

May 16, 1987. Commenting on having gotten $6 million in salary and bonuses since 1984, Tammy Bakker says, "We don't get what Johnny Carson makes, and we work a lot harder."

"READ! MY! LIPS! NO! NEW! TAXES!"

GEORGE BUSH

their sanctuary was being overrun by Republicans in pink and green Lacoste leisure wear (collars up) and red, white, and blue parasols. The Stepford delegates.

Swindle had a plan. We would plaster our way through the city, from the Quarter to the Superdome, in a scientific zigzag pattern known only to him—tacking from one bar to the next. The schedule called for one bar per hour. The teams loaded up their assault vehicles. We settled into the trashed Cougar;

Patti in full battle gear, a photographer from *Newsweek*, his lighting assistant, and another local photographer. Because the car had no radio or tape deck, Swindle brought along a boom box and a selection of tapes he had made off the sound boards of local piano lounges. Dr. John—live, Professor Longhair—live, and the most elusive, most eclectic of the lost New Orleans blues piano players, James Booker—LIVE! That car was like Tipitina's on

June 29, 1987. Meese discusses the Supreme Court vacancy: "We don't care about the political or ideological allegiance of a prospective judge." The audience bursts into laughter.

July 1, 1987. Reagan nominates Robert Bork to Supreme Court.

wheels. Swindle plopped his Saturn Bar "go-cup" cozy on the dashboard, settled his six-pack of Dixie beer between his legs, lit up a Taryton filtertip cigarette, and cranked up the boom box. It was Booker croaking, "Down the road came a Junco partner . . . he was loaded, loaded as can be . . ."

The closer we got to Ground Zero (the Superdome), the more police we saw. But we were entranced by a silver switching box on a median strip directly across from the Dome. It was a clear case of surface lust. Swindle pulled off to a side street. Patti and I went into "high-risk hit" mode. She walked a glue-soaked brush across to the median and swiped at the signal box. I stood on the other side of the street with a rolled poster against my side. The box whirred and clicked. The light changed, strobing Patti in midstroke. Tires squealed and sirens wailed. A squad car peeled around the corner. A heavyset city cop strode over to Patti, engaging her in conversation. I trotted over.

"Don't y'all know that we just spent five million dollars to fix up these streets so's they'd look pretty for the convention?" I told the kind officer—Officer Bourgeois, if my adrenaline-drenched eyes were reading his nameplate correctly—that we had come from Los Angeles to put up George Bush posters. Perhaps we were a little overenthusiastic. Officer Bourgeois wasn't buying it, and he hadn't even seen the poster. "You mean to tell me y'all came all the way from California to deface our fair city?" he asked, bemused. Patti chirped up, " Officer, we're so excited to be here. I think New Orleans is beautiful, and look at my wonderful George Bush "Republican Integrity" button!" Say what? The dear woman peeled off her black leather jacket and thrust her giant button in his face. It was pinned directly in the middle of the target on her Public Enemy T-shirt. She must have bought it in the airport when I was stuck at baggage claim. Officer Bourgeois didn't have a chance. He just chuckled, shook his head, and, walking back to his squad car, muttered, "Yeah, you right. Just get off my beat with that stuff, shugah!"

July 7, 1987. North testifies that he shredded documents in front of Justice Department officials, and that if the President ordered him to "go stand in the corner and sit on his head," he would do so.

July 10, 1987. Meese acknowledges adviser's Wedtech ties but denies ever discussing them.

September 30, 1987. Documents show FBI compiled files on more than 100 top U.S. writers.

WE'RE
ALL
ONE
COLOR
STOP THE KILLING

Fred Jones called me about fifty times in two weeks. Fred had an idea for a poster. Fred had grown up in South Central L.A. He was a black man who was very concerned about inner-city kids killing each other in gang turf wars over drugs. Crips and Bloods. He wanted an image for his slogan, WE'RE ALL ONE COLOR—STOP THE KILLING. Fred hoped to reach the gangs on their own turf: graffiti postering in the 'hoods. I told Fred (many times) that I was just a little white Jewish guy from Venice. Fred said he'd bring some gang members over to the studio to educate me.

Fred brought the kids. We went to the 'hood. I met Big Mike, Green Eyes, Minor the Major, and TECH, the master tagger. I learned. Gang-banging cost 425 young lives in L.A. County in 1988. These kids are not

"If the killing keeps going, they won't have to worry about the banging because there won't be nobody left."

J O H N (''Green Eyes'') H U N T E R

November 18, 1987. Iran-contra committee's final report ascribes ultimate responsibility to Reagan for failing to carry out oath to "take care that the laws be faithfully executed."

October 23, 1987. Bork's nomination rejected by Senate, 58–42.

1988

January 7, 1988. Records reveal Bush regularly attended meetings on Iran arms sales.

a drug cartel. They're stuck between a rock and a hard place. On one side, a flourishing drug trade that's a grotesque of the American tradition of enterprise capitalism. On the other, mean streets stripped of hope by a government that slashes funds for public education.

Soul handshakes are creative ritual greetings symbolizing societal membership. Welcoming to those who know the code, but also a form of insulation from an exploitive and hostile mainstream culture. They look cool and get the message across.

Whenever I have a design problem, I go whining to Debbie. She clears the kitchen table, pulls out her Magic Markers, tells me to sit down and be quiet—and solves the problem in five minutes. Fred and I went directly to Kitchen Table Graphics. Fred was pleased with the results. But I wasn't going to paint those handshakes. Photomontage was the only answer.

Fred got his teenage nephews, Timothy and Ed Jones, to dress in gang colors and jewelry; one as a Crip, the other as a Blood. He drove them out to Venice from their home in the Crenshaw district. The parking lot was directly across the street from photographer Al Shaffer's studio. We crossed the asphalt duck fashion: Al leading the way, me, Fred, Fred's daughter, Racquel, who was along for the ride, and the two boys. A journey of forty feet. Once in the stu-

dio, we looked around for Timothy and Ed—gone.

We peered around the corner. They were spread-eagled against Al's building, hands up. An unmarked police sedan was up on the sidewalk, pinning the boys to the wall. They were being frisked by two of LAPD's finest. The cops shouted obscenities in the boys' faces. Fred is a big man. That afternoon he was decked out in his LA Raiders gear—silver and black jersey, silver and black cap, and black Bermuda shorts. Fred got very big—and charged right through me. Fred yelled at the cops. The cops yelled at Fred. They threatened to arrest him. He threatened to arrest *them*.

The scene was drawing quite a crowd, and it was getting ugly. Suddenly, Al showed up on the corner, waving his $5,000 camera. His high, nervous voice pierced the din. "Excuse me, officers. These young men are professional models for a photo shoot of an *antigang violence* poster. You have them up against my studio wall. They should be inside, doing their job." Both cops turned whiter than they already were. Fred was livid. Timothy and Ed said it happened all the time in their neighborhood.

Fred's network of ex-gang members, church groups, and block organizations distributed the posters to inner-city neighborhoods around the country. You can even see one in Duane's room on "A Different World."

January 13, 1988. Supreme Court grants public schools broad powers to censor school newspapers, plays, and school-sponsored activities.

January 30, 1988. Abortion counseling barred at federally aided clinics.

February 21, 1988. Jimmy Swaggart temporarily steps down from ministry after confessing on TV to visits with prostitute.

"I hereby swear and undertake that if confirmed, during the course of my tenure as Secretary of Defense, I will not consume beverage alcohol of any type or form."

JOHN TOWER

May 8, 1988. Officials claim Bush heard drug charges against Noriega in 1985; Bush says didn't see reports until '88.

May 16, 1988. Supreme Court rules police may freely search through garbage bags outside private homes without warrant or reason to suspect criminal activity.

SEX   **DRUGS**   **ROCK & ROLL**

"**G**ood old boy" is an oxymoron. George Bush, the pork rind cowboy, picked John Tower as Secretary of Defense. Another oxymoron. Secretary of Offense would be more like it. For years, the women on Capitol Hill had to defend themselves against him. Bottles of Jack Daniel's cowered in his presence! Lee Atwater, chairman of the Republican National Committee, had just masterminded the dirtiest, nastiest election campaign in modern memory—politics as character assassination. Another good old boy. Atwater, who thought of himself as a rock'n'roll guitarist, added insult to injury by jamming with B.B. King.

The mantra of my generation is "Sex, drugs, and rock'n'roll." I'm still proud to say I was a hippie. I grew up with rock'n'roll—Ray Charles to the Rolling Stones. How could I resist the warped irony of joining that phrase to portraits of John Tower, George Bush, and Lee Atwater? If some people think my greasy rendering of Tower with SEX scrawled under him is a "safe sex" poster—so be it. If anyone still thinks Bush had *nothing* to do with Manuel Noriega's deals in Panama, or knew *nothing* about Iran-contra, maybe we deserve what we've gotten. And for those who thought of rock'n'roll as the devil's music but couldn't recognize the true face of evil—Lee Atwater. This time I could print a triptych, all three posters—make amends for my failure to have begged, borrowed, or stolen the money to print HEAR SEE SPEAK.

"Patti Party" organized a trip to Chicago. Her pal, John Cusack, had a theater company there, the New

May 31, 1988. Review of Justice White's opinions reveal belief that striking workers do not have right to subsidized food stamps and former alcoholics may be denied VA benefits.

Criminals. He offered to be our tour guide. The walls of the New Criminals' rented storefront rehearsal studio were lined with my posters. Glue buckets were strewn everywhere. We felt right at home. Except for the twenty people in outrageous period costumes prancing around—women in ratty, flowing gowns; men in frayed, turn-of-the-century three piece suits and bowler hats (one character had glowing saffron-yellow teeth).

I gave them my little guerrilla etiquette song and dance. Perhaps because they use their psyches and their bodies as their creative instruments, actors have more energy than anyone I know. By midnight, the Criminals had formed hit crews, divided up the town, and disappeared into the hot summer night—in costume! I could imagine these ghosts swooping around Chicago, all flowing gowns, glowing teeth, and flying glue brushes.

We agreed to meet at the Green Mill jazz bar around 3:00 a.m. My crew and I straggled in late,

"If everybody connected with politics had to leave this town because of chasing women and drinking, you'd have no government."

BARRY GOLDWATER

around four. Our night had been like Beetlejuice taking a driver's education class with Super Dave. Getting stopped for speeding through an illegal left turn at a stop sign, into a one-way street the wrong way, distracts from postering. Especially when the cop sees glue buckets and pictures of George Bush with the word DRUGS in the back seat. Anyway, the

July 18, 1988. Counsel McKay decides not to indict Meese, though acknowledges he "probably violated the criminal law" four times since becoming attorney general.

July 22, 1988. Wedtech prosecutor calls Meese "a sleaze."

August 12, 1988. Meese resigns as attorney general.

Green Mill was jumping. Three beers later, I found Patti sitting up on the bar, Fishbone cap backwards, calling out tunes to the band. I guess we loved Chicago.

Elizabeth Shepherd, curator of the Wight Gallery at UCLA, had set me up with a feisty group of Chicago artists for the next night's raid. They were a little annoyed with the Chicago City Council. It seems a student at the Art Institute had put a painting in the graduate show that the city fathers disliked. Ex-Mayor Washington in a tutu. Several councilmen had rushed down to the gallery and *arrested* the painting. Tore it off the wall. The government can't do that to art. It was payback time. By night's end, the artists had put up so many posters around Chicago, it looked as if the new mayor, Richard Daly, had declared SEX DRUGS ROCK & ROLL Day!

Since those days, both John Tower and Lee Atwater have died. When Bush had palpitations in

May 1991, I got calls from all over the country asking if I was moving up from guerrilla art and into voodoo—and if so, could I stick a few pins in some dolls for them? People even sent me dolls with names of public officials on them. Ouch!

"I'm not going to concentrate on being kinder and gentler ...because I'm not."

LEE ATWATER

"BUSH SUFFERS SHORTNESS OF BREATH DURING A JOG AND IS HOSPITALIZED— IRREGULAR HEARTBEAT DETECTED; CONDITION IS STABLE."

NEW YORK TIMES, May 5, 1991

George Bush picked Dan Quayle as his vice-president for two reasons: to cover his far right flank—Quayle is the scion of the ultra-conservative Eugene Pullian newspaper empire—and to clone a sycophant. Of course, Quayle brought a bonus package with the deal: impeachment and assassination insurance. Finally, we had a leader of vision. A prophet: "A thousand points of light"—as in tons of bombs and billions of dollars lighting up the oilfields of Iraq and Kuwait. "Read my lips. No new taxes." Now that's voodoo economics. Welcome to the recession! And Dan Quayle: George Bush's first thought bubble. The nineties are the decade of expedience. I have seen the future and it's for the birds.

   Mad magazine was the intellectual journal of my youth. I remember *Mad*'s brilliant riff on IBM's ubiquitous invocation, "THINK." *Mad* went with "THIMK." The success of IBM's simplistic dictum had spawned a series of corporate-style Zen zingers. *Mad* dissed them all! I admired *Mad*'s riffs on "BE NEAT" and

August 16, 1988. Bush picks Dan Quayle as running mate.

September 4, 1988. Candidate Quayle reveals comprehension of foreign affairs: "Perestroika is nothing more than refined Stalinism."

September 11, 1988. Bush campaign aide Fred Malek resigns after revelation resurfaces that in 1971 he prepared under Nixon's order a list of Jews in government bureaus.

PLAN AHEAD

"PLAN AHEAD." "BE NEAT" became a besmudged, fingerprint-sullied caricature of corporate earnestness. "PLAN AHEAD" was transformed into a scrunched ironic visual contradiction. AHEAD didn't fit in the space allowed. Kind of like Dan Quayle—except that in the *Mad* version, the space wasn't big enough to accommodate the word. In Dan's case, the man isn't big enough to accommodate the space!

Lenny had moved to New York. His loft was strategically located between SoHo, Little Italy, and Chinatown. I mailed 1,500 posters ahead of me, directly to the loft. I have "guerrilla wranglers" in each city we poster—volunteers who sit on the phones, coordinating our teams. In New York, we had traditionally gathered at Fanelli's bar on Prince and Mercer at midnight (of course). But the guerrilla network expanded to include progressive organizations like Refuse & Resist, the Rainbow Lobby, and ACT UP—among others. We outgrew Fanelli's back room. Besides, they had 86'ed us after SEX DRUGS

September 24, 1988. Reagan pocket-vetoes stricter ethics rules.

September 17, 1988. Nancy Reagan revealed to continue to receive free designer clothes, despite 1982 announcement that she would not accept them anymore.

September 21, 1988. Barry Goldwater advises Quayle, "Go back and tell George Bush to start talking about the issues."

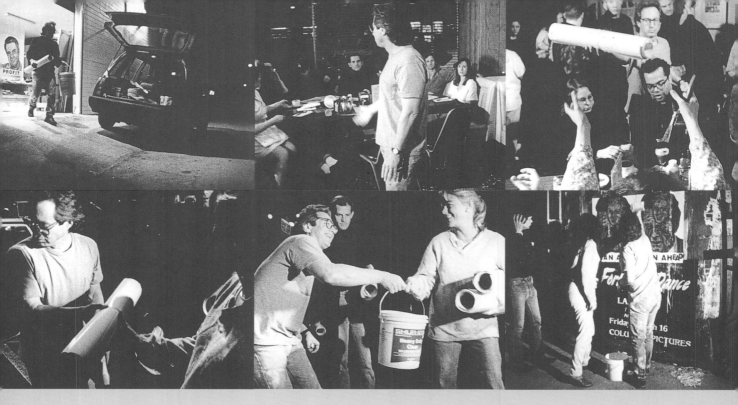

ROCK & ROLL. Something about too much glue in the beer.

To make sure we remained inconspicuous, we now had a documentary film crew following us around—lights, camera, action! Maybe they're why a middle-aged civil servant in a brown uniform steered an unmarked midnight-blue Ford Escort into a giant stack of overflowing black plastic garbage bags at the corner of Lafayette and Prince at 3:30 a.m. Walkie-talkie in hand, he asked me politely for my driver's license. "I'll have to cite you for every poster you've put up, young man. I am the Poster Police." My head did a 360-degree swivel. I saw hundreds of movie posters, garage band ads, obscure performance notices, Gupta Yogi Swami handbills, and stickers advertising a bewildering variety of unmentionable activities. I said, "I'm just an artist visiting from Los Angeles. Do you mean to tell me that every poster at this intersection is illegal?" By this time, the whole crew was giggling, and our graveyard shift street theater had drawn an audience. Five homeless people were eagerly awaiting the Poster Policeman's retort. Finally he said, "Everything is illegal, sir." The street people knew that was true. Our film crew asked if he would please speak into the microphone—this encounter was going to be broadcast on TV in the fall. The Brown Shirt hesitated. "Oh, okay, never mind. Just don't do it again." Our audience applauded. Several offered to help us poster—for a small fee. I was about to take them up on that when I realized one of them had strolled off with our glue and brushes and the rest of our posters.

September 25, 1988. In Dukakis debate, Bush names three weapons systems already cut from budget when claiming "there's plenty of weapons" he opposes.

November 8, 1988. George Bush elected president.

November 17, 1988. Bush names Lee Atwater chairman of the Republican party.

"DAN QUAYLE IS A MAN OF THE FUTURE."

GEORGE BUSH

December 1, 1988. Quayle decides to choose his words more carefully, since discovering that "verbosity leads to unclear, inarticulate things."

1989

January 12, 1989. Pat Robertson is quoted in *Rolling Stone*: "Lee Atwater has used every dirty trick known to mankind."

February 1, 1989. Witness testifies seeing John Tower drunk and out with women other than his wife.

"ANTI-HELMS BILLBOARD UP,

DOWN,

February 27, 1989. Tower pledges on TV not to drink if he's confirmed.

March 3, 1989. Senator Simpson says Tower is being "pecked to death by ducks."

March 6, 1989. Tower says he's being put through the worst meat grinder in Washington, and "I'm not even coming out coarse ground, I'm coming out fine sausage meat."

Federal funding of the the arts, or more accurately, the threat of withholding that funding, is being used to intimidate artists into producing "politically correct" art. Here, in America. This is embarrassing. Of course we should know by now that art isn't above politics.

If we're surprised by how much political hay Senator Jesse Helms has harvested by cutting an old-fashioned flattop out of the long hairs at the National Endowment for the Arts—then we haven't been paying attention for the last ten years. Whether it's Helms, or Senator Robert Dole chilling funding of the Corporation for Public Broadcasting because of its "liberal slant," or Tipper Gore and Susan Baker legislating song lyrics, these people should have a surgeon general's warning sticker on their rear ends: "Harmful to the Health of the First Amendment, the Future of Art in America, and Rock'n'Roll."

Jesse Helms was attacking ART. For me, this time it was personal! His idea was that certain citizens should not be allowed to make art with government funds. A subcitizenry of taxpayers, I guess. Certain subjects were not suitable for art supported by government funds, no matter how valid the art.

Homosexuality and art with homosexual content were "obscene." What the Nazis categorized as "degenerate art." Hey, they burned books as well as people. Wait a minute. The Stealth bomber cost U.S taxpayers more than *1 billion* per plane. The whole budget for the National Endowment for the Arts for fiscal 1990 was $171 million. That's obscene!

I whipped up something special for Jesse. I saw a giant prune face, with the hole where his brain should have been lined up exactly with the thumb-hole in an artist's palette, and (uncontrollable) gooey paint dripping down onto his forehead. A billboard would do the trick.

I found myself sitting across a large desk from a guy in a sharkskin suit, pinkie ring, and a cigar. The idea was to rent a billboard for the three months leading up to the North Carolina senatorial election. But heaven forbid I should bore anybody—could I change the text on the board each month? He said,

AND UP." NEW YORK TIMES
August 18, 1990

March 10, 1989. In first Cabinet veto
since 1959, Senate rejects Tower, 53–47.

HOLY HOMOPHOBIA!

"Sure, for a price. Whaddaya have in mind?" So I tried, "HOLY HOMOPHOBIA!" Something Robin might say to Batman after a bad day at the office. The shark with the cigar puffed, "Isn't that a blood disease?" I explained. He said, "Oh, it's a dirty word." I was crushed. Debbie had designed such a beautiful Olde English *H.* I whined, "So I guess you wouldn't go for CHRIST, I'M PISSED." He snorted, "Well, you can't use CHRIST, and PISSED is a no-no, but I'M would be okay." I took my last shot. "How about ARTIFICIAL ART OFFICIAL?" His eyes crossed. He had no idea what that meant—I knew I had him. "As long as it isn't controversial. We wouldn't want to offend anybody."

The billboard went up and for seven days all I got were compliments. "Nice likeness." "Big, isn't it?" "Love the yellow, Rob." Debbie had done a terrific job translating the painting into that awkward 14'x48' shape. But I was depressed. Maybe I had lost my touch—this honker wasn't offending anyone! But on the eighth day . . . the national office of the billboard company sent a one-sentence urgent fax to L.A.: "You have one hour to take it down." I felt much better. "Controversy" is a mild word for what transpired during the next two days. It turned out that 3M actually owned the space, and someone from Minnesota called offering to organize a national boycott of Scotch tape. This was sticky stuff! We even made 3,000 crack 'n' peel stickers. Most of us understood when Harvey Gantt asked us not to invade North Carolina—he was too nice a man (or maybe just too smart).

The company got so much adverse publicity for censoring an anticensorship message that within thirty hours of its removal they changed their little minds and put it back up. It got me some swell PR, another round of 100-phone-call days, and even two consecutive articles in the *New York Times*. Whew! This project had been just about the most excruciating art experience of my life. I vowed never to do anything legal again.

As John Frohnmeyer and most of the NEA's budget ride off into the sunset together, let's not forget that state support of the arts has always been political. By definition. Art has always been a potent cultural weapon. That's why politicians want to control it, sometimes for worse, sometimes—surprisingly—for better.

Take, for example, Michelangelo's David, arguably the greatest sculpture in Western art of a full male nude figure. It was funded by the city-state of Florence. It would not, needless to say, be a project Jesse Helms and his confederates would throw money at today. They're more into Stealth bombers.

When the Medici were expelled from the Republic of Florence in 1494, they repaired to Rome and plotted with their allies, Cesare Borgia and his father, Pope

March 13, 1989. Students occupy building at Howard University, forcing Atwater to resign from school's board of directors.

April 1989. During his Pacific tour, Quayle tells Samoans, "Happy campers you are, happy campers you have been, and, as far as I'm concerned, happy campers you will always be."

Patrick
mond AV 201
Come to where the flavor is.
FILTER CIGARETTES
HOLY HOMOPHOBIA!
SURGEON GENERAL'S WARNING: PREGNANT WOMEN WHO SMOKE RISK FETAL INJURY AND PREMATURE BIRTH.

QUEER NATION
HAS NO

FOR SALE
925-7778
WIRE WORKS
497
BELT GUARDS
WIRE PARTITIONS
WINDOW GUARDS
AIDS IS
HOLY HOMOPHOBIA!

Alexander VI, to regain control of the little city-state. The campaign reached crisis proportions in 1501, when the Republic commissioned Michelangelo to make a large sculpture to send a message of defiance. The David (Florence) would do battle with Goliath (the Medici and the Pope in Rome). The sculpture was so inflammatory that Florence had a shed built so that Michelangelo could work on it in secret. A meeting was held in Florence on January 25, 1504, to settle on the sculpture's placement. The minutes of this extraordinary gathering still exist in the *duomo* in Florence. Leonardo da Vinci and Sandro Botticelli attended. Tensions were high—the location had enormous symbolic significance. Out of nine suggested sites, the decision came down to in front of either the Palazzo Vecchio or the Loggia dei Lanzi. If the David were in front of the Palazzo, with his *terribilitá* scowl facing Rome, the Medici were sure to get the message. Placed in a niche at the Loggia, its political implications would be relatively neutralized. After a heated debate, the group decided to go for the jugular.

The situation was so combustible that on May 14, 1504, when the sculpture was ready, the leaders of Florence decided it should be installed at night. During its journey from the shed to the Palazzo, Medici supporters stoned the sculpture, knocking off David's middle finger.

Sound familiar? Maybe part of the problem these

June 6, 1989. Supreme Court eases burden on employers in some bias suits.

July 3, 1989. Supreme Court restricts right to abortion and gives states wide latitude for regulation.

April 20, 1989. Chief Counsel Nields, contradicting Bush, says key documents regarding Bush's involvement were withheld from Iran-contra panel.

WE'RE
ALL
ONE
COLOR
STOP THE KILLING

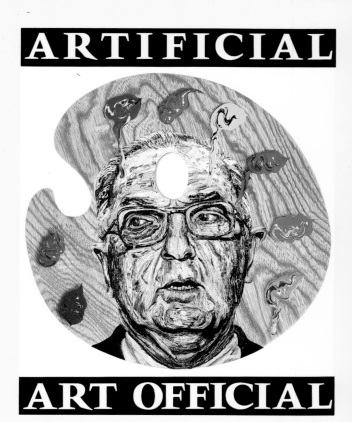

ARTIFICIAL

ART OFFICIAL

DAMAGE
CONTROL

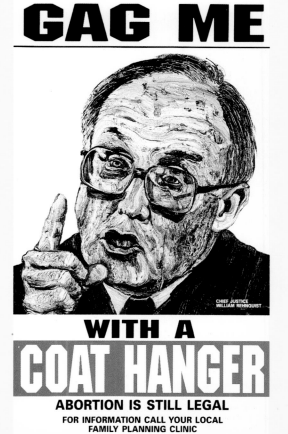

GAG ME

CHIEF JUSTICE
WILLIAM REHNQUIST

WITH A
COAT HANGER
ABORTION IS STILL LEGAL
FOR INFORMATION CALL YOUR LOCAL
FAMILY PLANNING CLINIC

Art Attack. HarperPerennial. © 1992 by Robbie Conal.

ARTIFICIAL ART OFFICIAL AUGUST 1990

"If I am re-elected to the Senate, God and the people of North Carolina willing, you ain't seen nothin' yet." (Jesse Helms, October 25, 1990)

Art Attack. HarperPerennial. © 1992 by Robbie Conal.

WE'RE ALL ONE COLOR JANUARY 1989

"If the killing keeps going, they won't have to worry about banging because there won't be nobody left." (John "Green Eyes" Hunter, January 22, 1989)

Art Attack. HarperPerennial. © 1992 by Robbie Conal.

GAG ME WITH A COAT HANGER FEBRUARY 1992

"Patients in clinics should not expect comprehensive medical advice." (Chief Justice William Rehnquist, July 3, 1989)

Art Attack. HarperPerennial. © 1992 by Robbie Conal.

DAMAGE CONTROL SEPTEMBER 1991

"Verbosity leads to unclear, inarticulate things." (Dan Quayle, December 1, 1988)

"IF I AM RE-ELECTED TO THE SENATE, GOD AND THE PEOPLE OF NORTH CAROLINA WILLING, YOU AIN'T SEEN NOTHIN' YET."

JESSE HELMS

days is that we've been taking our artistic license for granted. Look who's been doling out those grants lately—and who's got the power to revoke that license. When artists receive funding, it's our job to know where all the strings attached lead to. When some agency tries to jerk strings, we have to know how to string along the jerks. Or not. What happens when art runs a stop sign? Our license is history, right? We're only a roll of the dice away from "Go Directly to Jail. Do Not Collect $200."

If Jesse Helms has his way, the arts in America will be sentenced to Disneyland. Sometimes even artists have to fight back. If a huge statue of a naked young man showed up on Capitol Hill, scowling directly at Helms's office, do you think he'd be upset? What if a confederation of artists, graphic designers, and printers pooled talents and resources to provide *pro bono* promotional services to progressive organizations? We could place lively art about social issues in movies, music, TV, and the print media. This is sexy stuff. It could sell a lot of Reeboks. Oops—all we really need is consciousness.

When the Corcoran Gallery in Washington, D.C., yielded to conservative pressure and pulled the plug on the so-called obscene Robert Mapplethorpe photo exhibit, it took artists about two minutes to figure out that if they boycotted that institution, it would have nothing to show. No art, no NEA, no David. Just Goliath. Maybe that's what Goliath wants.

ARTIFICIAL

ART OFFICIAL

January 6, 1990. Costa Rican prosecutor links Americans to May 1985 fatal bombing, alleging initial investigations were hampered by local police "with close ties to the U.S. Embassy."

February 4, 1990. A CNN-*Time* poll reports that nearly two-thirds of respondents think Quayle unqualified to be president.

49

April 29, 1990. A *New York Times Magazine* article reveals that the Iran-contra committee intentionally limited its scope to avoid possibility of impeaching Reagan.

July 20, 1990. D.C. Court of Appeals overturns North's Iran-contra convictions.

September 25, 1990. Privately funded putting green is installed in Quayle's official residence.

Angelenos talk about everything in movie terms. Imagine a plot for *Terminator 3*: Arnold comes back from the future, even more domesticated than in *Terminator 2* (in which he "learned" to shoot to maim, not to kill), settles in Los Angeles, and quickly becomes chief of police. Wait a minute. Who needs Arnold? We have Daryl Gates!

One of my art students, Patrick Crowley, was upset by Gates's statement, "Casual drug users ought to be taken out and shot." Patrick had had several unpleasant run-ins himself with less than sympathetic police. He took Gates's fascistic statement personally. Gates brought us SWAT teams and the urban assault vehicular battering ram. His mouth is a loose cannon. He has informed us that Blacks' windpipes are "different from normal people's." Blasted KABC-TV anchorwoman Christine Lund, calling her "an Aryan broad."

Patrick brought me a sketch of Police Chief Gates's head superimposed on a copy of a rifle target. We worked for months. The best master silkscreen printer in L.A. offered to run an edition of 100 prints for free, on one condition—anonymity. Uh-oh. A sign of things to come.

Then Daryl Gates's officers beat Rodney King to within an inch of his life for speeding under the influence of a quart of Olde English 800 malt liquor. I rushed over to the silkscreen shop, picked up a blue grease crayon, scratched a line through SHOT, and scrawled in BEATEN. We could just barely keep up with the nightly news.

Anyone who has spent any time on the streets of L.A. knows the LAPD's reputation for brutality. Daryl Gates and his testosterone are proud of it. But police brutality is a national problem.

John Heartfield was a German agitprop photomontagist who put posters of Hitler, "Adolf the Superman, Swallows Gold and Spouts Junk," all over Berlin in 1932. In 1933, he jumped out of his apartment window, just before the SS jumped all over him, and escaped to Prague. TAKEN OUT AND SHOT became an homage to Heartfield—throwing Gates's words back in his face, right under his nose!

This was going to be our most clandestine action

October 2, 1990. Senate confirms Supreme Court Justice Souter, 90–9.

1991

January 16, 1991. Persian Gulf War begins.

February 3, 1991. Quayle inadvertently reveals on BBC location of U.S. Air Force's Stealth bomber base in Saudi Arabia.

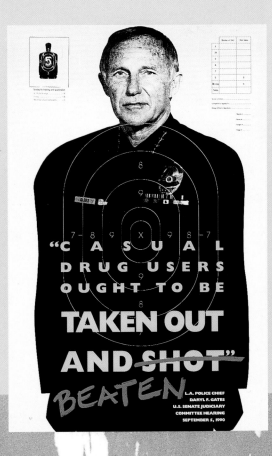

"C A S U A L
DRUG USERS
OUGHT TO BE
TAKEN OUT
AND ~~SHOT~~"
BEATEN

L.A. POLICE CHIEF
DARYL F. GATES
U.S. SENATE JUDICIARY
COMMITTEE HEARING
SEPTEMBER 5, 1990

yet. The first rule of guerrilla tactics is, don't attack the enemy head-on. If I went straight at the source of power, I'd be squashed like a bug. But my crack troops were hot to trot. I made my one tactical mistake. We went straight downtown to City Hall and the top cop shop in L.A., Parker Center. Like moths to a flame.

We spent an hour slipping between the raindrops. So far, so good. Suddenly, a black-and-white spotted us *and* the posters. I saw the driver go to his radio. Patrick, Patti, and I had one killer whale on our tail, steam rising off its hood about a block behind us. This was eerie—no flashing lights, no approach. I knew we shouldn't boogie—Rodney hadn't done so well with the high-speed chase thing. The squad car stopped at a traffic signal box. A cop in a Darth Vader rainslicker and hood went up to the box and gently stripped off the portrait of his chief. Everywhere we went that night the cops followed—quietly, at a distance—peeling down every poster we put up. Maybe they're art collectors.

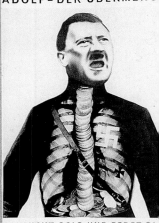

ADOLF – DER ÜBERMENS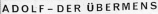

SCHLUCKT GOLD UND REDET BL

BE

51

March 2, 1991. As head of Competitiveness Council, Quayle orders EPA to give factories greater latitude to increase emissions without telling affected communities.

March 3, 1991. In Los Angeles, Rodney King is severely beaten, shot with a stun gun, kicked and struck between fifty-three and fifty-six times with batons, with twenty-seven uniformed LAPD officers present.

The summer of 1987 was great. There was a mini-series running on network TV, "The Iran-Contra Hearings," and on cable superstation WGN, the Chicago Cubs pitched, hit, and ran themselves right out of the cellar in the National League East. To paraphrase Harry Caray, "Double Holy Cow!" I was literally painting by remote control. And doublespeaking of remote, as I watched Oliver North and his "potted plant," Brendan Sullivan, whispering to each other on national TV, I kept getting flashes of my first political memory.

Spring 1954: I was back from baseball camp—walking two weeks' worth of dirty laundry up from the bowels of Grand Central Station in New York. That temple of transportation's fifty-foot-high glass wall spilled steaming shafts of light down onto one exhausted little shortstop below. I looked up and saw flickering black-and-white images on TV sets mounted high in the corners of the rafters. Maybe it was the Damn Yankees getting shut out once again by the awesome Cleveland Indian pitching staff. Hey kid, welcome back to the real world. CBS was broadcasting the Army-McCarthy hearings, *live*. There were Senator Joe McCarthy and his spoiled-child prodigy, Roy Cohn, whispering to each other, hands over microphones, in front of their largest audience ever. Trying to bully the army—as they had the American public—in the name of national security.

Summer '87: North and Sullivan—McCarthy and Cohn. They looked *exactly* alike! Either Ollie was channeling "Tailgunner Joe" or we had a virus within our democracy; one that erupted every decade. The fifties brought us McCarthyism—witch hunts in America in the name of national security. The sixties were Johnson's escalations in Vietnam—making the other side of the world safe from communism and

March 22, 1991. Publishing experts say LAPD Chief Gates may lose $300,000 book deal if he is no longer in office.

March 10, 1991. *Los Angeles Times* poll reveals majority says police brutality is common.

devastating a generation of young Americans. The seventies produced Watergate—Nixon and his henchmen spying on everyone; the evil spirit of his realpolitik haunts my whole lifetime. And Iran-contra was the eighties definition of foreign policy. Our statesmen? An "off the shelf" team of covert operators keeping the world safe from communists, Congress, and the American people.

Proust had his *madeleine*, I had TV. I'd paint a cautionary tale of two eras, warning people that representative democracy may be the rhetoric, but the mafia is the prevailing model for stuctures of power in this country. Abuses of national security doublespeak in the fifties poisoned our national character and ruined thousands of Americans' lives—in the eighties, it killed thousands of Central Americans, and should have brought down the presidency.

It took me a year to finish those paintings. Once completed, the 8'x15' monsters kept howling at the door of my studio, trying to get out. How could I get them onto the streets? Another billboard might do

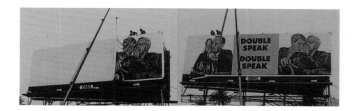

the job. By this time, my work was a real bother to the bureaucracy of the City of Los Angeles. The Public Works Department had once even threatened prosecution if I didn't promise to take down everything I'd ever put up and never, never do it again. I've always had this little problem with authority, and I don't make promises I can't keep—so they did the job themselves, and sent me a bill for $1,300. I paid it—they did good work, after all. Maybe I could convince L.A.'s Cultural Affairs Department that I now wanted to participate in the cultural discourse of the city on a higher plane: *above* the streets! I wrote up a proposal—would Cultural Affairs jump at the chance to get me off the streets? Yes! The city put up

April 23, 1991. Supreme Court upholds rule curbing abortion counseling at public clinics.

April 10, 1991. *New York Times*/CBS poll indicates 62 percent worry about Quayle as president if something happens to Bush.

June 23, 1991. More than two-thirds interviewed in *Washington Post* poll could not name any of the Justices of the Supreme Court. Fifty-four percent could name the judge on TV's "People's Court."

"DON'T TELL ME WHAT THE CASE IS, TELL ME WHO THE JUDGE IS."

ROY COHN

"I DON'T ANSWER ALLEGATIONS, I MAKE THEM."

JOE McCARTHY

$10,000. After several midnight-hour crises—it seems that certain City Council members didn't want DOUBLE SPEAK in their districts (too close to home?)—we put up the billboard on the Salvadoran side of Wilshire. Its "erection" was broadcast live on local TV, touching off a minor media firefight. Not because the issue of DOUBLE SPEAK was so controversial. Heavens no! The *Los Angeles Times* editors, various city officials, and AM talk radio call-in shows' switchboards were lit up by the idea that the Cultural Affairs Department would give 10,000 simoleons to a "vandal."

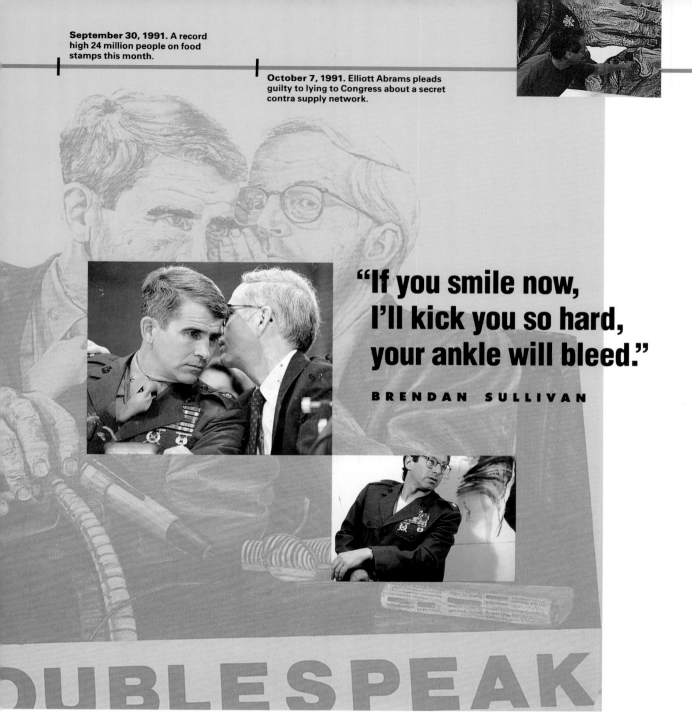

September 30, 1991. A record high 24 million people on food stamps this month.

October 7, 1991. Elliott Abrams pleads guilty to lying to Congress about a secret contra supply network.

"If you smile now, I'll kick you so hard, your ankle will bleed."

BRENDAN SULLIVAN

DOUBLESPEAK

"I think I shredded most of that. Did I get 'em all?"

OLIVER NORTH

"PEOPLE THAT ARE
REALLY VERY WEIRD
CAN GET INTO
SENSITIVE POSITIONS
AND HAVE A
TREMENDOUS IMPACT
ON HISTORY."

DAN QUAYLE

November 6, 1991. House passes bill overturning Bush's rule prohibiting abortion counseling in federally aided clinics.

November 7, 1991. Senate rejects abortion counseling ban, 72–25.

October 15, 1991. Senate confirms Supreme Court Justice Thomas, 52–48.

Even in politics, everyone has his limits. Dan Quayle is mine. I never thought anyone could outdo Spiro Agnew, with his "nattering nabobs of negativism." The guy clearly had a forked tongue. But Quayle stood up before 1,000 of the best-educated, most powerful Black people in America and said, "What a waste it is to lose one's mind, or not to have a mind is being very wasteful." Well, he should know.

Don't think I'm just talking about veeps *qua* veeps. Richard Nixon was a vice-president. Lyndon Baines Johnson, Gerald Ford, and George Bush were vice-presidents. Thirteen—count 'em—thirteen vice-presidents have become president, one way or another. But when Bush hurled chunks in the Japanese prime minister's lap in Tokyo and slipped under the banquet table (that photo looked like Mao swimming the Yangtze for a moment, didn't it?)—I felt sick too. Sick to my citizenship.

It's not just that Dan-o is dumb-o—a direct descendant of Howdy Doody and Alfred E. Newman. I think he's Dan-gerous. A conservative ideologue's perfect front. And never mind Dan-o's golf score, let's check the rest of the foursome—who's he "linking" up with? Take his Competitiveness Council, designed to ensure that regulations made by federal agencies, like Environmental Protection, don't get in the way of big business. It functions behind closed doors. Representative Henry Waxman has said, "The council is acting as a nefarious secret kind of government, outside the constitutional and democratic processes for enacting laws." Sound familiar?

Debbie loves San Francisco, so we went to do some DAMAGE CONTROL. Our troops were a wondrous assortment of performance artists and struggling filmmakers who worked nights as neo-hippie jewelry fabricators, nonprofit gallery denizens, club slime (in the sweetest sense of the word), and art rock musicians. Of course we headed straight for Haight Ashbury. In 1965, I lived in the Haight, in a storefront next to Kezar Stadium, while majoring in psychedelic drugs and cafeteria coffee at San Francisco State College. My hippie pals and I would climb up to our roof on Sundays to have macrobiotic picnics, smoke dope, and watch the '49ers.

Frisco is a fifteen-minute town. You can get anywhere on those toy freeways in a quarter of an hour. We roared through the wee hours, splattering glue to the sound of foghorns. The cops in the Tenderloin district thought we were advertising a children's play. Or we were children at play. I can't remember which.

We moved down to the financial district, circling the brokerage firms and fancy art galleries with DAMAGE CONTROL. A squad car with a bullhorn pulled up. "What do you think you're doing in this part of town?" I delivered my party line. "An art project, exercising our First Amendment rights, about choice in American politics." Uh-huh. A big blue man got out of the car, pointed due south, and lay down the law. "We have a place for this kind of stuff. Get out of the good part of town. Go south of Market, where you belong." I took a Rolaids and headed south.

December 1991. Republican senators stall bill authorizing $1.1 billion funding for Corporation for Public Broadcasting.

1992

January 2, 1992. George Bush throws up at a dinner in Japan.

GAG ME

CHIEF JUSTICE
WILLIAM REHNQUIST

WITH A
COAT HANGER
ABORTION IS STILL LEGAL
FOR INFORMATION CALL YOUR LOCAL FAMILY PLANNING CLINIC

Who picks candidates for the Supreme Court? The President. Who confirms candidates for the Supreme Court? Congress. Eight of our nine justices have been appointed by Nixon, Ford, Reagan, and George Bush. After *Rust* v. *Sullivan* and the confirmation hearings of Clarence Thomas, who could even *pretend* that the Supreme Court is above politics?

Many Americans were upset by the Court's ruling that doctors in federally funded family planning clinics were not allowed to mention the word "abortion," to their patients. Something about citizens' constitutional rights and women's rights to control their own bodies, I believe. The only good to come of the national debacle of the Thomas hearings is that none of us could ever forget the image of that Senate

Judiciary Committee—fourteen old white men—staring down at Anita Hill. Either they misunderstood her on purpose or they had no clue. Take your choice—and shove it.

Debbie kept after me about choice, the Court, and "Uncle Thomas." I resisted painting the Court—haven't I done enough ugly old white men? And all those black robes—yuck! It would turn into an imitation of Rembrandt's *The Dutch Masters*. Sounded great to Debbie. Uh-oh. The good news was that I only had to paint six of the nine: the five who upheld the "gag rule" and Clarence. Then she came up with a great line: FREEDOM *FROM* CHOICE. Which is just about what they've left us with. I ordered a ton of black and white oil paint and got to work.

But I was angrier than FREEDOM FROM CHOICE. I'd had enough of the Supreme Court in the last few months to last me my whole lifetime. Unfortunately, this Court *would* last my whole lifetime. I thought, "Gag me with the Supreme Court!" Uh-oh, Spaghetti-O's. How many GAG ME's could I think of? Six. Rehnquist: GAG ME WITH A COAT HANGER. Scalia: GAG ME WITH A SPECULUM. Souter: GAG ME WITH FORCEPS. White: GAG ME WITH RHYTHM. Kennedy: GAG ME WITH A PRAYER. And the punch line,

"Constraints that restrict an indigent woman's...freedom of choice are the product not of government restrictions on access to abortion, but rather of her indigency."

CHIEF JUSTICE WILLIAM REHNQUIST

February 26, 1992. Patrick Buchanan bashes PBS for showing a "pornographic and blasphemous" documentary on Black gays.

March 3, 1992. Department of Public Social Services study shows welfare caseload in L.A. County has increased 51 percent since 1988.

FREEDOM FROM CHOICE

Thomas: GAG ME WITH A (LONG DONG) CONDOM. Not nice. No more Mr. Nice Guy. There are so many bad guys, and so little time . . .

The next day I got a call from an acquaintance associated with the Greater Los Angeles Coalition for Reproductive Rights—a loose confederation of 100 pro-choice organizations. She wondered if I had thought about doing a poster about the gag rule. Could she and three officials of the group come over and try to talk me into a project on the subject? Faster than you can say "*Rust* v. *Sullivan* did not significantly impinge on the doctor-patient relationship, because patients in clinics should not expect comprehensive medical advice" (like Rehnquist did), I was surrounded by four of the nicest, smartest, angriest middle-aged women I'd ever met. They picked GAG ME WITH A COAT HANGER. I tried to talk them out of it. "Maybe it's not the most appropriate phrase for your constituency? Too aggressive, perhaps?" They laughed at me. Raised the money to

O'Connor rips radical feminists

GOD IS A MAN

print it in one week. Gathered up a veritable army of "guerrilla matrons"—and blasted off in their Volvo station wagons and spandex jogging suits to plaster Beverly Hills, the Pacific Palisades, Brentwood, and "Gourmet Gulch" on Montana Ave. in Santa Monica. They were terrific! Got 6,000 GAG ME's up from San Diego to L.A., the Bay Area, and Sacramento. The next week they were back. Wanted to translate it into Spanish. A thousand got printed. The ladies jumped into the closest telephone booths, donned their spandex gear—and vrrooom!

The next week they were back again! Asked me about FREEDOM FROM CHOICE. They knew more women from Planned Parenthood who were interested in a poster for the April 5 Pro-Choice March on Washington and some billboards for later. Could Debbie and I get the art ready? They would raise the money. Whew! All I can say is, the male politicians and powermongers of America better pay attention. Sisterhood is Powerful!

March 3, 1992. Jury picked in Ventura County for Rodney King beating trial. There are no Black members.

It's 1992, and we're watching *Back to the Future IV.* Reagan, Bush, what's the difference? Just "stylin'." After eight years of sniveling obse-quiousness, Bush had one original thought of his own. Dan Quayle. Let's do the man justice, Bush has actually had *four* original thoughts in four years: Quayle, John Tower as an example of excellence in the Defense Department, the Persian Gulf war (or how to kill 200,000 people, spend $100 billion, and not get the job done), and Clarence Thomas. For that matter, would a Democrat, say Michael Dukakis, have been any better? I doubt it. But that's not my job. I'm a guerrilla satirist. If they abuse their power, they're all fair game. I'd love to play pin the tail on the donkey, but they'll have to win an office worth aiming at first.

It's very difficult to maintain a truly critical position in our society. Without a well-honed sense of humor, it's impossible. Things just get too grim. While I have no illusions about the power of American culture to absorb any form of resistance, including mine, I think humor pro-vides a way of operating within the cracks and fissures of the system. Which is where I've been all along—falling through the cracks. Some fool once asked me my "career goal." You call this a career? I'd have to say that when I grow up, I'd like to be Christo's evil twin. My first project would be to place a giant condom over the Washington Monument, to remind our leaders to practice "safe" cultural imperialism. Jesse Helms and his confederates, who've declared cultural civil war on the rest of the United States, might like that. Maybe I could get a grant from the National Endowment for the Arts!

"SO MANY BAD GUYS, SO LITTLE TIME."

ROBBIE CONAL

Acknowledgments

There are so many people to thank for their help, encouragement, and patience with me and my "guerrilla mania." More than I can list, or remember. Robin Williams said, "If you can remember the '60s, you weren't there." Which goes double for all the postering we've perpetrated. Thanks to all of you. Especially:

My great pal, Danny Bradlow (happy fourteenth birthday!). Lenny Silverberg and Noni Reisner (happy wedding!). Franny Alswang. Ralphie Alswang. Joe DiMattia. Jonathan Salk and Elizabeth Shepherd. Leon Golub and Nancy Spero. Erika Rothenberg. Sue Coe. Jerry Kearns and Judy Arthur. Betsy Hess and Peter Biskind. Steve, Camille, and Marios Kerpen. Paul Slansky (my encyclopedia). John Berley. Janice Felgar. The irrepressible Al Shaffer. Holly Jones. Glenn Gastelum. Fred and Terry. Mel McCombie. Jennifer Foote. Ann Seiber. Hudson. Greg Green and Peter Taub (Go Cubs!). Jon Cohen and Shannon. Jane Greenstein. Margie at the Midnight Special. All the Vidiots. Jim McHue. Raymond Roker. Robert Berman. Dennis and Liz at Mirage. Karl Bornstein. Tom Schnabel and Ariana Morgenstern (for all the great music). Margaret Black. Be Be Crouse. Joan Hyler. Antoinette Bill. Judy James. Candace Van Runkle, of the L.A. Chapter, Friends of the Christic Institute. Mimi Maxwell. Charlie Sheen. Karen Dawneagle. Paul Haas. Paper Tiger TV. Aleks Mantelzak and Wendell Riggins. The Great Patti McGuire. Cathy Landis. Tim Robbins. Fast Al Nodal. Mike and Linda Swindle ("Choich iz Out!"). James Booker. Mike Luckovich. Heidi Schulman. Fred Jones. Tim and Edward Jones. Leon Watkins. Fishbone. Irv Weller. John Cusack. Jeremy Piven. All the "New Criminals." Garry and Jim (for the midnight ride). Jeanne Dunning and the guerrilla artists of Chicago. Joel Schumacher. Donna Dare. Doug and Sydney of the Daily Planet. Judy Jorrisch. Connie Julian and Lister. Paul Bartel. Deborah Irmas. Harry Montgomery. Tom ("Sure Shot") Simmons. Bill Heron. The Pasadena Art Alliance. Ken Coplon. Riley Forsythe. Chuck Philips. Hooman Majd. Jordan Peimer. Michael Jackson and Lyle Gregory. Patrick Crowley. Jeff Wasserman. The two Kevins. Toby Michel. Gary Nichols. Jan Williamson. Dolo Brookings. Ruella, Lupe, and Cultural Affairs. Don Redding. Judy Pollack and Barbara Patterson. Jayne Baum and Sam. Molly Rudder. Michelle Eisenberg. Clare Baren and David Dwiggins. Lynn Alvarez. Mary Jane Wagle. Cydney Mandel. Suzanne Campi. Marie Paris. Jamie Angell. Michele Mattei. Ragnars Vielands. Clay Walker and Marianne Dissard. Bette Talvacchia. Bill Luckey and Eileen Campion. The indomitable Stephanie Taylor. Tyrone. And, most gratefully, thanks to Christina Chang, Wendy Wolf, Susan Grode, and Debbie Ross, my partner.